Survival Skills

EXPRESS

Survival Skills Express

Survival Skills
EXPRESS

Know How to Prepare for Common
Disasters at Home and Learn Survival Skills
to Survive in the Wild on Your Own

Scott Graves & KnowIt Express

N2K Publication

ISBN 978-1-534-66829-4

Printed in the United States of America

First Edition

Welcome to the *Know It Express* - the express lane to knowledge!

To stay up-to-date, please be sure to sign up for **our newsletter** at http://www.KnowItExpress.com and follow us on social media:

https://www.facebook.com/KnowItExpress
https://twitter.com/KnowItExpress
https://plus.google.com/+KnowItExpress

Survival Skills Express

EXPRESS LANE

CHAPTER 1

Preparing for the Unknown

The Art Of The Unexpected

Survival is our most <u>primal core motivation</u>. We eat, sleep, fight off disease, and avoid unnecessary risks to survive, procreate, and pass on our genes. It's all about survival—for ourselves and for our genes.

But as you know, life is *unexpected*. Things can happen that change your life completely and immediately, sometimes for the better, but often for the worse. There's no way to escape such events, but you can prepare yourself.

That is why fundamental survival knowledge and skills are *crucial*.

A Survivalist's Philosophy

Why do you want to be a survivalist?

Knowing you can survive **without** modern society gives you a sense of self-sufficiency and satisfaction. You can take care of yourself without everything being handed to you in a convenient package. And so, when life takes an expected turn, you won't panic. You'll *know* what to do.

Staying **prepared** helps you stay calm in the face of enormous challenges or even disasters. Panic can blow things out of proportion, overwhelming your brain with hopelessness and inaction. On the other hand, when you are calm, ideas will begin to pour into your head.

So let's consider the best ways to prepare yourself for various disasters.

CHAPTER 2

Emergency Preparedness at Home

Disaster Management

Do you think, just because you're living a nice quiet life in your suburban neighborhood, *you don't need survival skills?*

Have you considered that fire could engulf your home? A wildfire could sweep through your area or a sudden electrical failure could start a fire from within. What about a hurricane or a major flood? What if thieves target your home?

Anything can happen at **any** time. Disasters do not respect your personality or time. *You are not in control.* But you can be <u>prepared</u>.

Flooding

Water is a necessity of life, but when it overflows, it can devastate properties and threaten lives. And sadly, it sometimes takes *only minutes* for this to happen. Heavy rain, strong winds, and tides all contribute to increased risks of flooding. So a hurricane near the full moon can cause severe damage. Even an earthquake in the middle of the river or sea can cause flooding.

How to survive a flood: Find or make a way to allow the water to <u>drain</u> elsewhere. Construct a good drainage system around your home that won't be overloaded by large volumes of water. It doesn't have to be an expensive, elaborate project. If nothing else, a series of hand-dug ditches that lead to major drainage channels is enough. Depending on the water level and velocity of the water, all preventive measures could fail and at this point, you need to get to **higher ground**. Know your local geography and pay attention to the weather warnings to determine what the risk is and how high you need to go.

Fire

Fire outbreak is a perennial problem in some regions of the world. In fact, some environments, like savannahs, burn periodically as part of their natural cycle. In modern times, humans have tried to suppress fire in some of these areas, but we've recently realized that this is only effective in the short-term and can have *disastrous* consequences in the long-term. Because when fire finally breaks out, there's more to burn and it's <u>much more dangerous</u>. Fires can also start *inside* your home, often due to an electrical failure (so replace old and fraying electrical cords).

How to survive a fire outbreak: The natural enemy of fire—we all know—is *water*. Soak a towel in water and use it to <u>cover</u> your face. This will protect your nostrils and eyes from the smoke, giving you a little longer to find your way out. If the fire is still young, you can try to extinguish it, but if it's already grown, <u>you need to get out</u>. To extinguish a fire, grab a fire extinguisher, and first pull out the pin! *Nothing* will happen with the pin in it. Then aim the nozzle at the flame, squeeze the handle, and sweep from side to side, covering the whole fire.

Earthquake

Certain continents, countries, and states are more familiar with earthquakes than others are. Places like Japan, Nepal, and California, for example, are at increased risk of earthquakes. But sometimes there are surprises, like the Virginia earthquake in 2011. Scientists are able to predict the risk of earthquake in an area and can often predict aftershocks or tsunamis, but they are *unable* to prevent earthquakes or give more advanced warning.

How to survive an earthquake: The vibrations of an earthquake are destructive: objects may slide off shelves, chandeliers may drop to the floor, walls may crumble, and roofs may collapse. Once the vibration starts, get *under* a strong material with an open base, such as a bed or table. Stay away from windows, bookshelves, and other things that might fall or shatter on you.

Accidents

Disasters aren't only natural, they can be caused by humans—others or yourself—and can follow you anywhere. Accidents can be minor (perhaps resulting in a shallow cut), moderate (perhaps dislocating a shoulder or elbow), life-threatening (causing organ damage), or even immediately fatal. They can happen inside the *house*, like spilling boiling water on yourself. They can happen on the *road*, slipping on ice or crashing into another car. They can happen in a *mall*, perhaps caused by a stray bullet from a criminal or the police. Despite the best laws, rules, regulations, planning, etc., accidents will happen.

How to survive an accident: Your plan of action will depend on the type of accident, but you must always consider <u>your own</u> physical condition. Check yourself for injury. Immobilize any broken bones and bind up any sprains with a bandage or cloth. For all cuts, the first thing to do is to stop the bleeding. Pressure on the wound will help, but if it's serious, also use ice packs or anything cold, which will slow your circulation. Covering the wound with cotton or wool will stimulate clotting. For deeper cuts, put pressure on the area with either or both of your hands and avoid moving, especially suddenly. The moment you move or try to, the muscular contractions will cause more bleeding.

The Art Of Prepping

So how can you prepare for any kind of emergency? This is the art of **prepping,** knowing exactly what to do when you have no electricity, running water, or heat.

You need to stock up <u>beforehand</u>. Most of the basics you should already have at home:

- first aid kit, with plenty of bandages and pain killers
- candles, lighter, matches, and firewood
- baby wipes (great for hygiene and staying clean if there's no water)
- paper towels
- battery- or crank-operated radio
- flashlight
- backup batteries
- can opener, all purpose knife, and/or Swiss army knife
- fire extinguisher
- some entertainment to pass the time when there is no electricity (board games, musical instruments, and books)

Some people advocate keeping a firearm, which can be used for self-protection or hunting. Be sure to follow your local laws and regulations. If you do own a firearm, *keep it safely away from children.*

Of course, two of the most important things are **food** and **water**. You should effectively have a food bank in your house, either in your pantry or perhaps down in the basement. Remember to keep an extra stock so that if the disaster hits at the end of the week, just before you'd usually do groceries, you still have enough to last for a while.

- WATER is essential to survival. A person should drink <u>8 cups of water per day</u>. One standard bottle contains 2 cups, so a case of 24 bottles, will last one person a week. A filtration system is also useful for when you have running water but it's been contaminated and *isn't drinkable*. If you have warning of a storm, you can set aside jugs or water to drink and fill bathtubs with water for cleaning or flushing toilets.

<u>Food</u>:
- canned fish or meat (Spam, tuna, salmon, chicken, turkey)
- canned vegetables (green beans, carrots, peas)
- canned prepared foods (baked beans, chili, and soup)

- peanut butter (nutritious, flavorful, and doesn't need to be refrigerated)
- oats, cereal, granola, or granola bars
- nuts and trail mixes (vacuum-packed for freshness)
- whole-wheat crackers
- dried fruits
- powdered milk
- sugar, salt, pepper, and any other easy flavorings
- rice, beans, and pasta (can be cooked in over a woodstove, outdoor fire, or even a few candles)

If you're a coffee person, consider an emergency supply of instant. It may not be the real thing, but it will be a whole lot better than nothing!

TIP: If your electricity is likely to return relatively quickly, try not to open your refrigerator. If it stays closed, the inside will remain cool and the contents won't spoil. If you think it'll be several days, it's better to eat the things that will spoil first.

Shopping For Food

To save money, buy in bulk. Instead of going to your local supermarket, go to a **warehouse** (like Sam's Club or Costco) and stock up.

There is no harm in stocking up, because if nothing bad ever happens, you can always eat the food and then <u>buy more</u>. But do be aware of the *expiration date* and don't let food go to waste!

Buy foods that you won't mind eating on a regular basis, not just in a disaster. Basically, you want to have a surplus of food so you're always prepared.

<u>TIP</u>: Try buying the **generic brands**. Why? Not only is it cost-effective, the shelf life is often longer. The more popular brands are more *expensive*, but are well known and often placed at eye-level, so they tend to sell better, while the generic brands sell slowly and so have longer shelf lives.

Of course, once again, you should always *check the expiration date.*

Storing Your Food

Have two stash piles: **active** and **reserve**. Keep the older foods and those with nearing expiration dates in the active stash. Put the newer purchases in the reserve stash.

The best strategy is to have a cycle period where you move over those reserve stash items over to the active stash, then **resupply** the reserved stash. This prevents older foods from going to waste, while also maintaining a <u>full stash</u>.

For larger food packages, like a bag of rice, store the food in smaller, **sealable** containers and put in an oxygen-absorber to maintain freshness. Consider portion size and the number of people in your family when choosing <u>appropriate</u> containers. This way, you can just grab one smaller package from storage while the others will stay fresh and ready. In addition, if you spill your bag or things spoil (especially meat), *only a small portion* is lost instead of the one large package.

Exercise: Build Your On-The-Go Survival Kit

Don't forget to prep for your daily transportation. You should always be prepared for an accident or a storm.

The following items should be kept in your car. **Customize** them however you like, so long as you have your bases covered. You can also simply buy a basic Gerber survival pack to keep in your car.

- GPS and maps (GPS is convenient, but electricity may be limited)
- insurance information and registration in glove compartment (always)
- bottled water
- Clif bars
- flashlight, candles, lighter*
- tool kit*

- backup cash (in case you lose your wallet or purse)*
- backup zero-balance credit card (for emergency purchases if not enough or no cash on you)*
- spare tire and tire changer
- extra gallon of gasoline
- blankets
- jump starter
- fire extinguisher
- rope*
- knife*
- car hammer or glass punch to break windows
- first aid kit and bandages*
- tape and glue*

*Note: The starred items should be put in a portable pouch (night light reflective) under your seat or in the glove compartment so that you can grab it all at once if you need to leave immediately (e.g. if your car is underwater).

CHAPTER 3

Surviving Out in the Wilderness

The Art Of Bushcraft

The world is an *unexpected* place, and disasters can happen to <u>anybody</u>. The chances of you ending up on a deserted island may be slim, but hiking accidents, plane crashes, boating disasters, and car accidents do all happen occasionally. And if you're in a more remote area, you'll need to be **prepared** to *help yourself*.

This is where the **art of bushcraft** comes in.

"Bushcraft" is a term for wilderness skills, knowledge that helps you survive away from civilization. To do that, you have to be *resourceful*, using whatever is available to meet your needs.

For example, a little <u>observation</u> will help you to identify useful objects and edible plants.

- A chipped rock can serve as a knife, a long stick can be sharpened into a spear for catching fish from the river, and sea sponges or leaves can be used for cleaning.

- You can observe the plants other herbivores eat and try them, in small quantities, until your innards get used to them.

So let's learn some bushcraft.

Starting A Fire

If you're going to survive cold nights outdoors, you'll need a fire. So you better know how to start one!

If you were in some sort of crash, the first thing you need to do is to <u>search the wreckage</u>. If you had a hiking accident, hopefully you held on to your pack and came well prepared.

It's easiest, of course, to start a fire with matches or a lighter. Fuel from the wreck may help too. If you don't have anything to start the fire, you'll need to do it with a spark.

First, gather dry leaves, grasses, and tiny twigs. Place them together to form a small heap that will catch the spark.

Here are two ways you can create fire:

a.) Find two rocks with rough surfaces. The best rock to use is **flint**, a rock historically used in weapons and for starting fire; it has a glossy or silky look with sharp edges, almost like broken glass. Some rocks may not produce a spark, so you may have to <u>experiment</u> with different rocks, especially those with a glassy, sharp surface. Hold the rocks close to the dry grasses and strike the surfaces against each other *just like striking a match*, hard and repeatedly. When you succeed in getting a spark, gently <u>blow</u> on it until a flame begins to blaze on its own. Then feed it with small twigs and then branches.

b.) This is known as the hand drill fire-starting method. Use friction between a stick and a plank of wood. Make a **depression** in the wood about the same size as the stick and put some dry grass or leaves around near it. Hold your hands together on the stick as you would if you were clapping, and spin the stick back and forth between your hands *quickly* in a downward motion. Then bring your hands back to the top and repeat this downward spinning hand-motion. When you start seeing smoke, you are getting close. The friction produces an ember. Add some dry grass and continue to blow or shake to get the fire going.

This is a lot harder than it seems on TV and it takes a while. You really have to practice to get a feel for it. So step outside your house and <u>try it now</u>.

Setting Up Camp

If you need to camp overnight, a <u>clearing</u> is better than the thick of the forest. A well-constructed **shelter** can shield you from danger and can *also* be used to bait and trap animals.

- Find four to five long **branches** about the thickness of your arm. They can be rough and of different lengths.

- Draw a circle on the ground and dig **holes** on the circumference for each of the wood logs that you have gathered.

- Shove the logs into the holes *at an angle* so that they will converge at the top, forming a cone.

- Keep them <u>in place</u> by stuffing dirt and stones around their base.

- Use twine, rope, or a strip peeled from the midrib of broad leaves like bananas to **tie** the top together.

- Tie flexible sticks **between** the upright branches.

- Use leaves to **cover** the branches. This will trap your body heat at night and provide some *shelter* from the wind and rain.

Acquiring Water

Scientists agree you can live up to 8 weeks without food, but you'll need water within *days*.

So the key is to find water before you go take care of your hunger. Water first, then food.

- Yes, we said water then food, but **fresh fruits** are actually a great source of water. Coconuts especially have a large amount of water. The younger *green* coconuts contain more water than browning ones.

- But obviously, you'll want more water than that, so look for *running* streams that aren't too muddy.

- Although moving water is more likely to be free of disease, it's always a good idea to **sanitize** your water if you can. If you have iodine tablets with you, they will kill the bacteria in the water. Fabric can also be layered to <u>filter</u> out mud.

- A great way to sanitize water is to boil it. All you need is a **container** and a **fire**. You may have to get creative. A waterproof fabric, seashell, or piece of wood carved inward by a knife for a bowl-shape might have to serve. If the container is flammable, place rocks in the fire to heat for a while so it can trap more heat inside and then place the hot rocks in the water, but be <u>careful</u> not to burn yourself.

Remember, start hydrating yourself *as soon as possible* so that you'll be ready to do everything else you need to do, like finding food and shelter.

Finding Food

Finding food may be a great challenge, depending on where you are and how familiar you are with that environment.

Two strategies for finding food are to kill animals or observe what they eat. Animal meat provides you with a good source of protein. But if you are not a good hunter, watch out for animals like rabbits and pigs because there is a good chance that you can eat whatever they do.

If you are lucky to be close to a river source, you can also try fishing with wooden spears or nets made from any available fabric or fibers.

Although a sick or wounded animal is easier to catch, if it looks <u>diseased</u>, you probably shouldn't eat it (e.g. if they give off dark blood or creamy discharge).

Plants are another, often more immediate food source. The question becomes whether they're **edible** plants. Remember that while many plants are not particularly palatable, only some are actually poisonous. **Avoid** any plants with milky sap or white berries, as these are more likely to be *poisonous*.

You can chew on some of the plants you encounter, but at first **don't** swallow them. Spit it out and judge the taste. If they cause an acidic, tingly sensation, you shouldn't eat them.

Once you decide to eat a plant, only swallow a small amount and wait half a day to see if you get sick. If you don't experience any problems, wonderful. If you do, avoid that plant in the future.

Remember you can eat the leaves fresh or cook them over the fire. You can also boil them to make soup/tea.

The taste won't always be pleasant, but it will be better than starving.

Two other, often overlooked, sources of nutrition—and especially protein—are **bird eggs** and **insects**. Most insects are edible raw, but it's safer to <u>roast</u> them. Worms, grasshoppers, crickets, and ants are all good options, so put aside your squeamishness.

Calling For Help

The ultimate goal, when you're lost in the wild, is obviously to be <u>rescued</u>.

With this in mind, it is advised that hikers carry a signal gun or some sort of mechanized location indicator. But let's face it: very few people actually follow this advice.

There are, of course, a few simple ways to call for help. (**Do not** use the fire method in areas that are susceptible to wildfire.)

- Gather dry twigs and grasses. Follow the instructions on <u>making a fire</u>. At night, the fire will attract attention itself. During the day, **smoke** is actually more visible, so feed the flame with *green* grass and branches that will produce smoke.

- Another method is to create three fires in a straight line, about a hundred feet from each other. This is a known **distress signal.**

- Use materials such as rocks, branches, and leafs to set up **symbols** like an "X" or words like "HELP" or "SOS" that might be seen from the air; you can also do the same in the sand. Ideally, you want to always keep these markings set up, so you don't have to hastily light your fire for every incoming plane.

- Use your belt, **reflective** metal, or a mirror to signal using the sun's light.

<u>TIP</u>: anything that looks *unnatural* will draw the attention of searchers.

<u>Exercise</u>: Build Your Wilderness Survival Kit

What we have discussed is a primitive form of bushcraft, but if you are prepared with survival tools, you can last a long time.

If you know that you're going out camping, have two survival kits: one with you and one in your car. Here are some survival tools every survivalist and bushcrafter should have in their survival toolkit.

- firesteel and striker (MUST-HAVE convenient tool that will immediately help you start fire without relying on the rocks or hand drill methods. Plus, unlike lighters or matches, they are never used up.)*
- multi-purpose pocket knife
- candles
- whistle (grabbing attention)*
- mirror and magnifying glass (can help with calling for help or starting fire)*
- duct tape (for binding things together such as shelters or spears)
- saw wire (useful for cutting tress and hanging things)*
- fish hooks and lines (just in case)*
- ropes (paracord is ideal)*
- iodine tablets (sanitizes water)
- Ziploc bags (storing food or water)
- compass*
- space blanket

*Note: For extra lightness and roominess, you can remove some of the starred items from your wilderness survival kit, by buying a survival bracelet or survival belt that already has these items built in all together as an everyday wearable bracelet or belt, like a James Bond secret gadget. When you finally need any of the tools, you take the survival bracelet/belt apart to retrieve them. (These are very popular among diehard survivalists, just as many people these days can't leave the house without their phone.)

Exercise: Venture Out To The Wilderness

Camping is a fun opportunity to both relax and gain hands-on experience being a bushman.

Here are three tasks you should try to complete on your own.

- Set up a camp
- Make fire without using a match or fuel
- Forge a spear

If you have kids, camping is a great way to pass down some important skills. If you're new to camping, however, you might want to practice and work out the kinks first, otherwise your kids might not enjoy their time in the wilderness.

CHAPTER 4

Extreme Primitive Living

The Art Of Homesteading

"I am prepared for the worst, but hope for the best."
- **Benjamin Disraeli**

Modern civilization relies so much on consumerism and infrastructure that most people wouldn't know what to do off the grid or in a post-apocalyptic world. Knowledge of **homesteading** and the ability to be self-reliant and self-sufficient can be both <u>valuable</u> and *rewarding*.

Obviously, you're unlikely to ever be in a situation where you have to resort to such extreme measures. But in times of disaster, these skills could be crucial. And in the meantime, you'll gain some useful knowledge that may even improve your **everyday** life.

Growing Your Own Food

Consider a situation in which you have to grow your own foods and maybe breed animals. Maybe you're lost in the wilderness with little hope of rescue, or maybe a natural disaster or war has overturned your state or country.

Obviously, you'll have to work with what's around you, and your options may be limited. However, you can grow food just about anywhere.

Gardening or farming skills are vital for survival in the worst-case scenario. Whether you're stranded somewhere for a month or the stores have been destroyed, what are you going to do when you're out of food? Grow your own sustainable food source, of course! Be a farmer.

Exactly what you should farm may depend on where you are, what seeds you have available, the season, and how long you plan to be there. For example, winter squash is easy to grow, but it's planted in the spring and doesn't mature until fall.

Here are some of the fastest vegetables you can grow:

- Radishes will be ready to harvest in about 1 month.

- Green onions (the roots take months to mature, but you can harvest the stalks after a few weeks)

- Lettuce and spinach can be harvested in about a month.

- Peas will sprout in 1-2 weeks and can be harvested after about 2 months.

What about fruits? Strawberries grow pretty quickly, but most fruits take a lot longer to grow, especially trees. Some of the fastest-growing fruit trees are figs, mulberries, and peaches, but they take at least a year to produce fruit. So if you are in an emergency situation, stick with vegetables.

If you have seed packets, read the instructions carefully because each type of plant needs different treatment and conditions. Pay special attention to the shade tolerance, planting depth, spacing, and watering instructions.

Off-The-Grid Survival

Strategies for surviving a few days off the grid differ significantly from long-term strategies. The mindset is different, and you'll have to adjust accordingly. For one thing, a safe shelter or residence is even more important. For another thing, you'll need to be careful not to use up a supply that may be **crucial** later on.

Returning to a primitive way of living is a challenge, but if our great ancestors could survive, you can too. Your body has an amazing ability to adapt.

Perhaps the most important thing is to <u>stay calm</u>. Don't waste resources or your own strength.

In particular, remember to:

- Salvage whatever you can;
- Have all the necessary tools in your bushcraft survivor kit and know how to use them;
- Keep some seeds at home, practice gardening, and carry a pack of gardening seeds with where you go.

Being alone can drive anyone nuts, so you'll need to keep up a positive attitude. Don't be afraid to talk to yourself or personify objects around you. You can create an imaginary friend as Tom Hank's character did in the movie <u>Castaway.</u> He named a volleyball "Wilson" to keep him company through his ordeal.

CHAPTER 5

Innate Survival Training

Conditioning For Survival

Eighty percent of survival has to do with attitude. Some people quit before the game starts. Having the right attitude will go a long way.

What it comes down to is training both your body and your mind. This training will serve you well in everyday life as well as in an emergency. The most important training can be broken into the following categories:

- Determination
- Agility

- Stamina

- Strength

Determination

Simply put, determination is the will to succeed, or in some cases to survive. Determination nudges you on, even in the face of looming danger. It is the voice in your head that says "don't give up."

How to work on determination: Determination involves keeping your eye on the goal. Despite trying and failing repeatedly, with your eye fixed on the goal, you'll keep trying. And the more you do, the more the determination to keep trying *becomes a part of you.*

- **Role models** can help you build a sense of determination, especially ones who have experienced setbacks themselves.

- Consider taking lessons in **karate** or boxing to toughen you up a little bit and build up your determination.

- When you wake up, spend some time each day mentally preparing yourself for a disaster. Know what steps you will take. **Yoga** or meditation may help you do this while also building inner peace.

Agility

Agility simply refers to how swift and coordinated you are, for example, your ability to move quickly out of the path of oncoming danger. Agility isn't simply how fast you can run but how fast you can *respond*. Agility can be developed or improved through well-structured training sessions.

How to exercise agility: Your natural reflexes will help you to avoid danger. So part of agility training is teaching your body to listen to and use those instincts.

- <u>Sports</u> generally help you build agility. Different sports involve different skills: tennis and handball require hand-eye coordination, while football requires foot-eye coordination. So it's often a good idea to get some practice in a *variety* of sports, even if you mostly train in one.

- Agility training can be done alone, but it's both more fun and **more effective** with others. After all, you can't anticipate the movements of others as easily as your own. Play with your friends or consider joining a club where these games are played.

Stamina

Stamina is your ability to withstand sustained physical and mental pressure. Stamina allows you to withstand stressful conditions for a long time. Almost everyone can run a few hundred yards, or even a mile. But only if you train consistently, building up your stamina, will you be able to run a marathon.

How to build up stamina: Stamina will come naturally when you *repeat* a particular action and your body becomes used to it. Thus, any exercise targeted at improving stamina will be <u>all about repetition</u>. As the actions are repeated, your stamina will grow, and you will be able to overcome your previous limits.

- Athletes who want to improve their speed often tie a **weight** to their waist or legs and run with it, trying to keep up their former pace. When they have done this for a long time and the load is removed, running is much easier, so they are faster than before. You can borrow this trick, using anything that will make your everyday tasks *a little bit harder* and build your stamina.

- Use the stairs rather than the elevator and, if you have the time, try walking instead of driving sometimes. This will build up the stamina of your legs especially.

Strength

The simplest definition of strength is how much weight you can move. Strength is important for survival because you'll often have to move large objects, whether they're in your way or useful for something.

How to build strength: Like stamina, strength grows the more you use your muscles. The easiest way to build strength is to join a gym, but you can also exercise on your own. Remember to exercise all parts of your body, not just the ones that you enjoy exercising.

- Pull-ups are a simple home exercise. Hold a horizontal bar and try to pull your body up above the bar. Practice with your palms *facing* your head and *away* from your head. This strengthens

<u>different</u> muscles in your arm and will make it easy for you to carry and move heavy objects.

- Pushups can also be done easily at home. Just lie on your belly, place your palms on the floor under your chest, and push your body off the ground. If you can't do a single pushup, **don't worry,** you can start by letting some of your weight rest on your knees.

Eat For Fuel, Not Full

Not only is overeating bad for your health and overall fitness, but research has also shown that over feeding reduces your *mental* alertness.

It's especially important to avoid junk food and feel-good snacking. Eat more protein (particularly meat) and fruits, because those are readily available in the wild or off the grid.

In a disaster situation, you're unlikely to have enough food *every* day, so you'll have to <u>ration</u> it. Learn to eat just enough to keep you alive and **strong enough** to do what needs to be done.

Eat *slowly* to allow the food to settle in your stomach and your brain to realize you've eaten. You'll find you feel full faster.

The Japanese have a philosophy called "hara hachi bun me" which involves eating only until your stomach is 80% full to avoid it *stretching*. Such stretching increases the amount of food you need to eat to feel full. This is especially important in survival situations.

Remember eat for fuel, not full.

CHAPTER 6

Survival Best Practices

Relax And Breathe

If you've been practicing and training as suggested, you are now ready to take on just about any survival situation. Here are a few best practices you should keep in mind.

Whenever you feel your heart racing, take a deep breath in and out. Do this repeatedly until your heartbeat stabilizes. This may sound juvenile, but it *actually works*, and that's all that matters.

A racing heartbeat is not good for your health. In particular, it can lead to high blood pressure and can exacerbate any other conditions that you have.

After composing yourself, you will be able to think more clearly about how to proceed.

Work With Your Environment

In a new environment, always look for possible <u>exits</u> in case of emergency.

Make friends with people in the neighborhood so that you will always have people to look out for you. Start by simply making it a habit to greet your neighbors and ask about their day.

As you become acquainted with your neighbors, let them know that you're there to help if they need it, and <u>they'll do the same for you</u>.

Start a garden behind your house. It doesn't have to be large or beautiful—after all, most flowers won't do you much good in terms of nutrition. Simply grow a few herbs, vegetables, and even fruits.

Not only will this give you **experience** that could be useful later, it may give you something to talk to those neighbors about! You can even *trade* tips or the products of your labor. Everyone loves fresh produce from the garden.

Maintain A Healthy Diet

Adjust your diet, eating only as much as you need, with a hearty nutritional balance. Consume less alcohol and any other substances that might limit your mental or physical agility. You need to stay <u>healthy and alert</u>.

Draw up a new **meal plan**. Keep your breakfasts and dinners light, consuming the *most* at lunchtime. The afternoon is when most of the hard work is done, so you will need <u>all the energy you can get</u>.

Be disciplined and *avoid* snacking, if possible (although a small snack to tide you over to the next meal is better than overeating).

Remember to eat simple foods such as those you'd find in **nature**, especially fruits, vegetables, and nuts.

CHAPTER 7

The New Survival of the Fittest

Always Be Prepared

Survival may seem to have a lot to do with luck, but what it comes down to is preparedness.

- Develop the necessary survival skills and make prepping a practice to prepare for potential disasters before they happen.

- Remember to build your strength, stamina, agility, and determination. Each is important, but *together* they will get you through many tough situations.

- Keep an eye on your diet, because a poor diet will affect you not just physically, but mentally and emotionally as well.

- Don't forget your survival toolkit. Carefully consider your travel. Remember that what you need may vary on your location and situation.

The Meaning Of Life

In the end, life is all about survival. It can throw unexpected hurdles at you one after another. How an individual handles these situations may determine their survival of the fittest level.

The good news is that anybody can increase their survival chances through their level of preparation.

So get acquainted with all the survival basics and practice the things you've been taught, and you'll always be ready to survive and thrive.

As a final note, attitude is key. Take the following to heart and you'll forever be a true survivalist:

- Be resourceful. Maximize every object in your environment.
- Be creative. Make a way where there seems to be none.
- Be bold. Don't be afraid to try.

Survival Skills Express

Now You Know!

We have now gone from - *NOT knowing*...to *KNOWING*.

Doesn't it feel great? As cliché as the proverbial saying goes: knowledge is, indeed, power. The more you know, the more empowered you become. Not knowing is defeating, as you succumb to feelings of helplessness and surrendering of your own self.

Of course, acquiring knowledge is a never-ending quest. There is a great saying by Nobel Prize French author Andre Gide: "Believe those who are seeking the truth. Doubt those who find it."

At the very least, we hope we have set you off in the right path in regards to what you have set out to know, and that you have enjoyed our little journey together for the time you have spent with us.

If you can tell us how we did, that would be very appreciated! We value your feedback and always look forward to hearing from you, or if there is any way we could improve the entire experience for you. If you have a success story, even better - please let us know!

http://www.KnowItExpress.com

Don't forget to stay in contact for we would love to connect with you.

https://www.facebook.com/KnowItExpress
https://twitter.com/KnowItExpress
https://plus.google.com/+KnowItExpress

What would you like to know? Let us know!

CONTACT US

Now onward for more power to you, and thank you!

Survival Skills Express